GLOBAL TRADE IN
THE ANCIENT WORLD

GLOBAL TRADE IN
THE ANCIENT WORLD

Tish Davidson

MASON CREST
PHILADELPHIA

Mason Crest
450 Parkway Drive, Suite D
Broomall, PA 19008
www.masoncrest.com

Printed and bound in the United States of America.

CPSIA Compliance Information: Batch #CWI2016.
For further information, contact Mason Crest at 1-866-MCP-Book.

First printing
1 3 5 7 9 8 6 4 2

Library of Congress Cataloging-in-Publication Data

on file at the Library of Congress
ISBN: 978-1-4222-3666-6 (hc)
ISBN: 978-1-4222-8121-5 (ebook)

Understanding Global Trade and Commerce series ISBN: 978-1-4222-3662-8

Table of Contents

KEY ICONS TO LOOK FOR:

Words to Understand: These words with their easy-to-understand definitions will increase the reader's understanding of the text, while building vocabulary skills.

Sidebars: This boxed material within the main text allows readers to build knowledge, gain insights, explore possibilities, and broaden their perspectives by weaving together additional information to provide realistic and holistic perspectives.

Research Projects: Readers are pointed toward areas of further inquiry connected to each chapter. Suggestions are provided for projects that encourage deeper research and analysis.

Text-Dependent Questions: These questions send the reader back to the text for more careful attention to the evidence presented there.

Series Glossary of Key Terms: This back-of-the book glossary contains terminology used throughout this series. Words found here increase the reader's ability to read and comprehend higher-level books and articles in this field.

The ruins of a marketplace in the city-state of Athens, in modern-day Greece. In ancient times, this area would have been filled with traders buying and selling goods.

The Origins of Trade

The bazaar in the central square of Samarkand is crowded with people arguing, negotiating, trading, and making deals. The year is 750 CE, and Samarkand (in modern Uzbekistan) is one of the most important cities in Central Asia. Here, many trade routes meet, including the famous Silk Route that stretches 6,400 miles (10,000 km) from China to the Mediterranean Sea. For hundreds of years, traders have stopped in Samarkand to buy, sell, or trade for goods that are in short supply in their homelands.

A caravan of two-humped Bactrian camels waits patiently on one side of the square. The camel handler gives a command and the lead camel folds its legs under it and settles on the ground waiting for its cargo of precious Chinese silk and paper to be unloaded. A string of donkeys that had carried cinnamon, perfume, and sandalwood from India is being loaded with ceramics, glassware, and engraved copper dishes to take back to India. A one-humped dromedary loaded with olive oil spits at a passerby who has come too close. A trader offers lapis lazuli from, Afghanistan to a merchant headed to Egypt where the stone is highly valued, while a pickpocket tries to rob the distracted merchant.

In the bazaar, Buddhists mingle with Zoroastrians, Nestorian Christians, and Muslims. Business is conducted in a dozen languages. Turks trade with Indians. Chinese trade with Greeks, and Egyptians trade with Uzbeks. Language, ethnicity, and tribal allegiance are not important so long as there is a chance to make a profit. A skilled and lucky trader can become fabulously wealthy.

Buildings surround the central square. A few are built in the old style using square bricks, but most are made of the oblong bricks introduced by the Greeks after Alexander the Great conquered the city in 329 BCE. Beyond the buildings, a complex system of irrigation canals supplies the city

Words to Understand in This Chapter

barter—to exchange things for other things instead of buying and selling using money.

city-state—an urban area protected by walls that had its own ruler.

resin—a sticky semi-solid substance similar to pine pitch that oozes out of some trees when their bark is cut.

tribute—protection money; money paid to keep from being attacked.

with precious water and lets farmers grow crops on land that would otherwise be too dry. The buildings and irrigation systems were built from the profits of trade.

The call to prayer rings out from a minaret. The bazaar quiets. Muslim traders stop to pray. And then, prayers finished, the trading continues as it has done for a thousand years.

The Development of Trade

Trading is a universal human activity that has occurred in every culture from the earliest of times. Trade is driven by the uneven distribution of resources such as minerals, plants, and animals. Salt, for example, is found in abundance in some areas and is completely absent in others. People in the ancient world traded for necessities, such as food and medicine. They also traded for luxury goods such as furs and silk because owning rare items from distant lands was a way to show one's wealth and status.

The earliest exchange of goods in the ancient world occurred through *barter*. Individual traders negotiated an exchange of products based on their estimate of equal value. There were no standard measures. A trader had to size up the quality and quantity of the goods he was being offered and determine what he would offer in return. Three barrels of olive oil might be traded for a dozen sacks of wheat. The trader might then travel to another village and barter his wheat for a length of woolen cloth that he needed to make a new shirt.

As trade increased, gold or silver became a more common and convenient form of payment for goods. Countries issued their own coins in different sizes and values, but gold and silver were universally accepted as payment. A trader who sold his goods for coins had more flexibility in what he could buy than a trader who had to barter for what he needed. Still later, systems of credit developed where merchants could acquire goods with the promise to pay later when they were sold.

Traders in the ancient world had many obstacles to overcome. First were the physical hazards of travel—snow-

About Dates and Calendars

Different cultures use different calendars to indicate historic time. In the recent past, Western (Christian) cultures have designated the birth of Jesus Christ as year 1. They used the designation BC, meaning "before Christ," for dates before year 1 and AD, meaning *anno domini* or the "year of our Lord," to indicate dates after the birth of Christ. This book uses the designation BCE or "Before the Common Era" instead of BC and CE or "Common Era" instead of AD as a neutral, non-religious way of dating events.

One thing to remember when reading ancient times is that for dates designated as BCE (or BC), the smaller the number, closer the date is to the present time. For example, 700 BCE is closer to the present than 1500 BCE. However, with dates designated CE (or AD), the larger the number, the closer the year is to the present time. For example, 1500 CE is closer to the present time than 700 CE.

Another confusing thing about dates is the naming of centuries. The seventh century BCE extends from the first day of 700 BCE to the last day 601 BCE. The first century BCE starts on the first day of 100 BCE and ends on the last day of 1 BCE. The first century CE covers from 1 to 100 CE. There is no year zero. We are currently in the twenty-first century, which began in 2001 and will end in 2100.

This detail from a Medieval European map shows a caravan traveling on the Silk Route. This network of trade routes made it possible for distant empires like China, Persia, and Rome to exchange goods and ideas.

storms, dust storms, flooded rivers, and roads that were little more than stony paths. Villages were far apart. Bandits on land and pirates on the sea waited to attack traders and steal their cargo. Rulers or tribes that controlled the trade routes often demanded *tribute* in exchange for safe passage through their lands. Added to this were cultural, religious, and language differences, disease, and wars that were sometimes fought to control trade routes. Still, thousands of years ago, goods managed to travel from China across Asia to Europe. Along with the exchange of goods came an exchange of ideas and technology that formed the basis of our modern civilization.

The Roman Empire at its height ruled a vast area of Europe, western Asia, the Middle East, and north Africa. Romans traded within the empire, sending wine from Gaul (France) in exchange for olive oil from Libya or grain from Campania or Sicily. The Romans also exchanged goods and ideas with civilizations outside their own, importing luxury goods such as spices, marble, silk, perfume, and ivory with merchants from China, Persia, India, and southeast Asia.

Making Trade Easier

Think how hard it would be to trade if you did not know how much a sack of grain weighed or a length of cloth measured. In the ancient world, each *city-state* had its own system of weights and measures. In Mesopotamia (modern Iraq, and parts of Syria and Turkey) a complicated system developed because there were no numerals (1, 2, 3) as we know them. Instead of a number followed by a symbol for an item, each item had its own symbol that combined the number and the object. For example, there would be a symbol for one sheep and a different symbol for two sheep and still a different symbol for one goat, but no separate symbol for the numbers 1, 2, 3, and so forth. Measuring lengths was a little easier, as many cultures used measurements such as a finger, hand, foot, or step. Each kingdom or city-state also produced its own gold and silver coins. Not only were these coins different weights and values, but the purity of the coins varied. In some places, for example, a silver coin was 92 percent silver and in others it was 87 percent silver.

The Romans eventually developed a widely accepted system of standard weights, measures, and coins, and took their standards to the countries they conquered. At its peak, the Roman Empire covered a huge area from modern England, through much of Europe, all the land around the Mediterranean Sea, and Bulgaria, Romania, Turkey and other parts of the Middle East. Over time,

Did You Know?

Amber is fossilized tree *resin* found in countries bordering the Baltic Sea (modern Lithuania, Latvia, and Estonia). Archaeologists have found amber beads in a Siberian (Eastern Russia) tomb from the 600s BCE that could only have reached Siberia through long-distance trade.

Roman standards gradually replaced local standards making trade among different parts of the empire easier.

How We Know About the Ancient World

Archaeologists are people who study ancient civilizations. They put together many pieces of information to form an idea of how people lived and what they valued based on clues these civilizations left behind. Experts often disagree on what specific clues mean, and over time, new discoveries can change the way they interpret these clues. Even modern scientific techniques cannot give the exact date when an object was made. However, with enough clues, it is possible for archaeologists to get a good idea of the routes traders followed and the goods they exchanged.

Some of the best clues to trade in the ancient world come from burial chambers. From the pyramids of Egypt to grave mounds in Siberia, many cultures buried objects of value in the tombs of their rulers. Since rulers were important people, the buried objects often include rare items acquired through trade. These provide proof that goods were exchanged between distant lands. Some tomb objects can be dated using a scientific technique called radiocarbon dating, also called carbon-14 dating. Radiocarbon dating only works on material that originally came from plants or animals such wool or linen cloth, bones, or leather. It does not work on metal, stone, or glass objects such as coins or jewelry. A carbon atom normally contains six neutrons and six protons giving it an atomic

Artifacts found during archaeological excavations, such as this one at Nessebar, Bulgaria, have indicated that trade between ancient human civilizations has thrived for thousands of years.

number of 12. Carbon-12 (C-12) is stable. A small amount of carbon-14 (C-14) is formed by collisions with cosmic rays from space. C-14 has six protons and eight neutrons, and is radioactive.

All living things take in both C-12 and C-14 from the atmosphere. When a plant or animal dies, amount of C-12 it contains remains constant, but the C-14 is unstable and breaks down or decays. The half-life of C-14 is 5,700 years, which means that in 5,700 years half the C-14 in an object will have disappeared, but the full amount of C-12, which does not decay, will remain. By measuring the ratio of C-12 to C-14, scientists can determine the approximate age of an object of plant or animal origin.

Information from radiocarbon dating is just one clue to when trade occurred in the ancient world. Few written records have survived, but the ones that do often are accounts or inventories of trade goods. In addition, early Greek and Roman historians wrote about their countries in ways that add another piece to the picture of trade. These writings are valuable, but because they were written long after the times they describe, they are not always accurate.

Products were not the only thing that traveled along

trade routes. New ideas about technology, art, and religion came along with the traders. For example, Mediterranean countries learned about papermaking and the production of silk from the Chinese, and both Buddhist and Islamic beliefs were introduced to new areas by traders. Studying the spread of ideas, artistic designs, and religion, adds another clue to trade routes in the ancient world. When all the clues are put together, scholars have developed a good picture of what, when, and how people traded long ago.

 ## Text-Dependent Questions

1. What is barter? Give an example of how barter works.
2. What are three problems traders in the ancient world faced?
3. Explain the difference between BCE and CE.

Research Project

Different cultures use difference calendars to mark the passage of time. Look up the Hebrew calendar, the Islamic calendar, and the Chinese calendar and determine what today's day, month, and year is in each of these calendars.

The ruins of Soluntum, an ancient Phoenician settlement on the coast of Sicily. The Phoenicians were the greatest seafarers of the ancient world, establishing powerful city-states around the Mediterranean Sea that were connected by commerce.

2

The Phoenicians

The Phoenicians were early seafaring people. They arrived on the coast of the Mediterranean Sea in what is now Lebanon around 3200 BCE. Historians do not agree on where these people lived before they settled there. Over the next 2,000 years, the Phoenicians developed their skills as boat builders and sailors. They became the greatest seafaring trading power in the ancient world. The high point of their power occurred between 1200 BCE and 800 BCE when they controlled trade in a large part of the Mediterranean Sea.

Geography is Destiny

In some places along the coast of Lebanon where the Phoenicians settled, the mountains drop directly into the sea, so that sections of coast are separated from each other. In

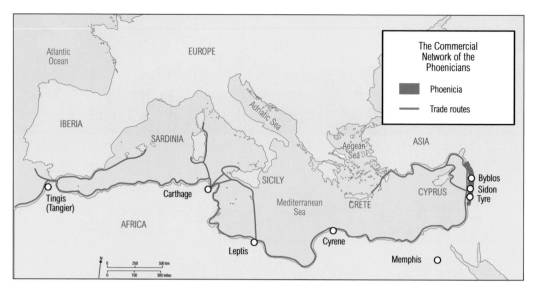

Atlantic
Ocean

EUROPE

The Commercial
Network of the
Phoenicians

Phoenicia

Trade routes

Adriatic Sea

IBERIA

SARDINIA

ASIA

Aegean
Sea

Byblos
Sidon
Tyre

Tingis
(Tangier)

Carthage

SICILY

CYPRUS

AFRICA

Mediterranean
Sea

CRETE

Leptis

Cyrene

Memphis

N

0   250   500 km
0   150   300 miles

ancient times, building trails across the mountains to con-
nect these isolated regions was difficult, so the Phoenicians
used boats to travel up and down the coast.

   With the mountains so close to the sea, land that could
be used for farming was limited. This caused people to live
close together in cities along the coast. Since many
Phoenicians depended on the sea to provide food instead of
farming, they became excellent ship builders, fishermen,

Words to Understand in This Chapter

export—to send goods out of a country.

flax—a plant whose fiber can be used to produce linen cloth and whose seeds can
   be pressed to extract oil.

papyrus—a paper-like material made from a plant that grew along the Nile River
   in Egypt.

and sailors. At first small Phoenician ships traveled short distances along the coastline, usually staying within sight of land. As navigation and shipbuilding technology improved, larger trading ships sailed throughout the Mediterranean from Greece to North Africa, and even to Spain. Some historians believe the Phoenicians also sailed through the Strait of Gibraltar that connects the Mediterranean Sea to the Atlantic Ocean and traded along the Atlantic coast of Africa. By 1200 BCE, the Phoenicians were a powerful international trading country.

Unlike many people in the ancient world, the Phoenicians were not part of a large empire controlled by a single ruler. Instead, each isolated section of coast developed its own walled city with its own ruler and its own cus-

Detail from a Roman mosaic shows Phoenician ships arriving in the harbor at Ravenna.

toms. These were called city-states. All the Phoenician city-states were on the coast, and the most powerful had excellent harbors.

Byblos was one of the earliest city-states. The city still exists, and is about 26 miles (42 km) north of Beirut. Byblos claims to be the oldest continuously inhabited city in the world, although a few other cities dispute this claim. In ancient times, Byblos was a powerful trading center because of its good harbor. Tyre, a city-state built on an island just off shore, had two good harbors, and became a wealthy and powerful port. Other Phoenician city-states included Berytus (Beirut), Sidon, which was a center of

Royal Purple

Royal purple was a dye produced in the city-states of Tyre and Arwad. The dye was prized because the deep purple color it produced did not fade when clothing was washed. The dye came from sea snails of the genus Murex that live in shallow tidal pools along the coast. The source of the dye was a thick gelatin-like substance that the snails secreted. Two other snails were used to make dark red and blue dyes, but purple was the most valuable color.

To make the dye, the snails were collected in large containers and crushed. Next, their flesh was left to rot for a few days. Ancient writers who recorded the way the dye was made complained that the rotting snails made the whole city smell awful. Salt and possibly other substances were added to the rotting flesh, and then the whole mess was boiled. Bits and pieces of shell and snail flesh were skimmed off the top of the boiling kettles. When no flesh was left, the liquid could be used to dye cloth or be boiled until only solid dye was left. The dye was so valuable that it could be traded for its weight in silver. Purple clothing was such an important status symbol that the Greeks and Romans restricted its use to royalty and high priests.

In the ancient world, cedar trees from Lebanon were prized above all other hardwood. Cedar wood was straight and smelled nice, making it a preferred choice for temples and palaces. It was especially valued in Egypt, where there was little hardwood available.

glass manufacturing, and Arwad, another island city-state. Phoenician city-states competed with each other for trade, but they did not go to war against each other. This helped the country prosper.

Early Sea Trade

At first the Phoenicians traded only products they produced themselves such as glass, dried fish, and lumber. Lumber was their most important trade good. The mountains that isolated city-states were covered with magnificent cedar trees. The cedars of Lebanon could grow to 130 feet (40 m) tall. The Phoenicians used cedar poles for ship masts and boards for shipbuilding. They *exported* the extra lumber to other countries.

Large parts of Egypt were desert where few trees grew, so the Egyptians had to trade to get wood to build ships, houses, and temples. The Egyptians also wanted resin from cedar trees to use as a medicine and to prepare the dead for mummification. Soon the Phoenicians were sending ships full of cedar logs, cedar resin, olive oil, and wine to barter in Egypt. In exchange they received gold, ivory, *papyrus*, and *flax*. This trade was so successful that soon the Phoenicians built larger ships that could sail farther, faster, and carry more cargo.

Development of Transit Trade

Transit trade is the transportation and trade of items that are not made or grown in the region from which they are shipped. Transit trade developed early in the ancient world. As you will read in later chapters of this book, great trade routes extended from China to the Mediterranean Sea. Some of the east-west caravan routes ended at the city-states of the Phoenicians. Here traders would unload goods from across the Middle East and even from as far away as China into Phoenician ships. The Phoenicians became rich on transit trade by providing transportation for goods they did not make.

The route lapis lazuli took from Afghanistan to Egypt shows how transit trade worked. Lapis lazuli is a blue stone that was highly valued in Egypt where it was associated

The blue gemstone lapis lazuli (below) was used for decoration throughout the ancient world. It provided color to the tiles on this Babylonian relief, as well as for the funerary masks of Egyptian pharaohs.

with the powerful goddess Hathor. The stone was in great demand by pharaohs and priests, but it was not found in Egypt. Lapis lazuli was mined (and still is today) in the Badkahshan region of northeastern Afghanistan.

At the Afghanistan mines, the stone was sorted and loaded on camels. Caravans made up of camels belonging to several traders would set off on one of the many trade routes that branched off the Silk Route. The Silk Route was the main trading path that linked China to the Mediterranean region. When the caravan reached a

city such as Samarkand (in modern Uzbekistan) where several trade routes met, the traders would barter lapis lazuli for goods coming from Mediterranean countries such as spices that had a high value in Afghanistan. The

Samarkand traders who acquired the lapis lazuli would join a new caravan traveling toward the Mediterranean Sea, and the traders who had acquired the spices went back to Afghanistan and sold their new cargo at a profit. The lapis lazuli would change hands this way many times in many different cities along the route before reaching the Phoenician city of Byblos. Each time it changed hands, the price increased.

In Byblos, lapis lazuli would be exchanged for spices, ivory, papyrus, linen, and gold that the Phoenicians had acquired on trading trips around the Mediterranean Sea. These goods would travel by caravan back toward Afghanistan. Lapis lazuli and other trade goods arriving in Byblos, such as, wine, silver jewelry, and copper items, went by Phoenician ships to Egypt, North Africa, and the Mediterranean islands of Malta, Cyprus, Greece, Sardinia, and Sicily. At each stop, these goods would be traded for spices, gold, and other items. Most of these trade goods would pass through Byblos on their way east by caravan toward China. The Phoenician city-states were able to become rich from the transit trade even though they made or grew only a few of the products they were trading.

The Phoenicians used large ships called triremes to carry goods throughout the Mediterranean region.

Trade Spreads Culture and Ideas

The Phoenicians are credited with developing the great great great great ancestor of the alphabet you are using to read right now. Today we write using an alphabet where each letter stands for a sound. Before this system was developed, people in the Mediterranean ancient world used two different systems of writing. Cuneiform (kyu-nee-eh-form) was a type of writing used in Persia (Iran) and Mesopotamia (Iraq, Syria, and Kuwait). Wedge-shaped marks were pressed into damp clay tablets in a certain pattern. Each pattern represented an object such as "sheep" or "man." To write in cuneiform, a person had to memorize hundreds of different patterns, one for each word.

The other system of writing was hieroglyphics, which were used in Egypt. Hieroglyphics used a combination of pictures and symbols to represent objects. This writing system was more flexible than cuneiform because symbols could be combined to form words. But hieroglyphics had the same problem as cuneiform. To read and write, a person had to memorize a large number of symbols.

The Phoenicians traded with people who spoke many different languages. They needed a way to record trade deals without memorizing thousands of different symbols. Their great advance was to associate each mark, or what we would call a letter, with a single sound rather than with an object. The Phoenician alphabet had twenty-two consonants but no vowels. Using these letters, they could write any word. Ordinary people could learn to read and write without having to study for years. This made recording trades and sending messages much easier.

The switch from using pictures to using letters for writing took many years to complete, but the idea was unstoppable. On their trading trips, the Phoenicians introduced the idea to the Greeks.

Did You Know?

As the Phoenicians' sea power grew, they established colonies that stretched from the North African coast to in western Mediterranean (modern Spain and Portugal). The largest colony was Carthage (in modern Tunisia). The Romans burned Carthage to the ground in 146 BCE and sold 50,000 people living there into slavery, destroying the power of the last Phoenicians.

The Phoenician alphabet (pictured below) differed from earlier writing systems like cunieform (above) because in Phoenician each symbol represented a sound, with symbols combined to make words. Phoenician became one of the most widely used writing systems in the Mediterranean world, and it was the forerunner of the modern alphabet.

Ruins of a Phoenician temple in modern-day Lebanon.

The Greeks later introduced their alphabet to the Romans, and the Romans spread the idea through their large empire that stretched all the way to England. Each culture made changes in the alphabet, which is why Greek looks different from Russian or English or Hebrew, but the concept of letters equaling sounds remains the same.

Decline of Phoenician Power

Phoenicia was a small land surrounded by larger powers. In 538 BCE, their land was conquered by the Persians. About this time, many Phoenicians moved to the trading colony of

Carthage that they had established in North Africa (Tunisia). About 200 years later the Greeks, led by Alexander the Great captured all the Phoenician city-state. From then on, Phoenicia was ruled by foreigners, and Phoenician culture disappeared. Today, the Phoenicians are remembered as the best sailors in the ancient world and, more importantly, for introducing their alphabet wherever they traded.

 **Text-Dependent Questions**

1. How did the geography of Phoenicia influence the Phoenicians to become traders?
2. What is transit trade?
3. How was the Phoenician alphabet different from cuneiform or hieroglyphics?

 **Research Project**

The Phoenician alphabet was the ancestor of both the Hebrew and the English alphabet. Look up the Phoenician, Hebrew, and English alphabets and make a chart comparing them. What are some of their similarities and differences?

A camel caravan moves across the Arabian desert.

The Incense Route

T he time is 300 BCE. A line of eighty one-humped camels, or dromedaries, belonging to Arab traders plod across the desert. They are loaded with heavy sacks containing a fortune in frankincense and myrrh (pronounced murr). In about three months, the traders will travel from the southern part of the Arabian Peninsula to Gaza (southern Israel) on the shores of the Mediterranean Sea following the Incense Route.

What is the Incense Route?

The Incense Route, sometimes called the Incense Road, was one of the most important ancient trade routes in the Middle East. It started in the highlands in what is now Oman and covered about 1300 miles (2100 km). After crossing through what is now Yemen, the route turned north in modern day Saudi Arabia and followed an inland route parallel to the Red Sea. At the northern end of the Red Sea, the route split. Some caravans headed across the Negev desert of the Sinai Peninsula to Alexandria, Egypt. Others continue north into what is now Israel. From there, the valuable cargo of frankincense and myrrh could travel by sea to Rome and Greece or by land following other trade routes into Mesopotamia (Iraq, Syria, and Kuwait) and Persia (Iran).

The Incense Route was not a road as we know roads today. Instead, it was a path through the desert used for hundreds of years. Along the way were about 65 *oases* and small villages roughly 20 miles (32 km) apart where traders could rest for the night and buy food and water for their animals. Experts disagree about when and how the route developed. Some historians believe it came into existence as early as 2500 BCE and that at first donkeys were used to carry goods along the desert route. Other historians believe that the route was not regularly used until about 1400 BCE.

Words to Understand in This Chapter

aromatics—substances that give off a pleasant smell.
domesticate—to tame a wild animal and keep it as a work animal or for food.
oasis—a place in the desert with water and plants.
tariff—a tax on goods coming into or going out of a town or country.
UNESCO—the United Nations Educational, Scientific and Cultural Organization.

They argue that the route became profitable for traders only when wild dromedaries were *domesticated* and could be used as pack animals. Historians do agree that the most important activity on the route occurred between 700 BCE and 200 CE. During this time, thousands of tons of frankincense and myrrh were carried north along the Incense Route each year.

Frankincense and Myrrh

The Christian Bible says that three Wise Men brought the baby Jesus gifts of gold, frankincense, and myrrh. We know what gold is and that it is as valuable today as it was in ancient times, but what are frankincense and myrrh? Why were they so important that they are mentioned more than one hundred times in the Hebrew Bible (Old Testament) and Christian Bible?

Pellets of resin from the Frankincense tree, which when burned give off a sweet, pleasant scent. Since ancient times, frankincense has been used in religious rituals and ceremonies.

A frankincense tree grows on a hillside in the Dhofar region of Oman.

Frankincense is a resin that oozes out of the Boswellia sacra tree if the bark is damaged. When burned as incense, this resin produces a sweet, woodsy odor. Boswellia trees grow only in Oman and Yemen on the Arabian Peninsula and Somalia in Africa. The tree has multiple stems like a bush instead of a single trunk, but it can grow as high as 25 feet (8 m). In ancient times, as well as today, the best frankincense came from Dhofar, Oman. Although much of the Arabian Peninsula is desert, the mountains in Dhofar block humid winds from the Arabian Sea. This creates fog that provides moisture to the trees.

Today frankincense is still harvested the way it was thousands of years ago. Shallow cuts are made in the bark of the tree. The resin oozes out and hardens into pebble-sized pellets called tears that harvesters chip off the tree. The tears are then sorted by color ranging from white (most valuable) to brown (least valuable).

Myrrh is also a tree resin. It comes from Commiphora myrrha, a thorny tree that grows to a height of about 13 feet (4 m). These trees are found in Yemen on the Arabian Peninsula and in Somalia, Eritrea, and parts of Ethiopia in Africa. Myrrh resin is harvested in the same way as frankincense and hardens into small yellow tears. In ancient times, almost all myrrh came from Yemen. Today most of it comes from Somalia. When used as incense, myrrh also produces a pleasant smell.

Like frankincense, myrrh is a tree resin. While sometimes burned as incense, myrrh had other uses. The Egyptians used the resin in the process of making mummies, and an oil extracted from myrrh was used for healing by many ancient cultures.

Camels on the Incense Route

Two types of camels were used on ancient trade routes. Bactrian or two-humped camels were used on the eastern part of the Silk Route. Dromedaries, or one-humped camels, were used on the Incense Route and the western part of the Silk Route. Without camels there would have been very little long-distance trade.

Dromedaries are one-humped camels that originated in the dry lands of the Middle East. They are perfectly adapted to life in the desert. They have tough mouths that allow them to eat thorny desert plants. Their long double eyelashes keep out the desert sands, and their feet, which have two toes, are covered with flat, leathery pads that let them move easily over the sand. Most importantly, they can break down the 80 lb (36 kg) of fat in their hump into water and energy, which lets them go without drinking for ten to fifteen days. When they do drink, they take in large amounts of water quickly.

People living along the Incense Route kept dromedaries for food, milk, and their hides and trained them to carry heavy loads. Once a healthy dromedary was six years old, it could carry 350 to 650 lb (159-295 kg) for a day and could carry 200 lb (90 kg) for 15 to 20 miles (24 to 32 km) day after day even in hot weather. Without dromedaries to carry frankincense and myrrh, and provide milk, meat, and transportation for traders, the Incense Route would never have existed.

Bactrian camels (left) and dromedaries carried goods on the Incense Route.

The Demand for Frankincense and Myrrh

Frankincense and myrrh were the most expensive and prized *aromatics* in the ancient world, equal in value to gold. In ancient times when people rarely bathed or changed their clothes, frankincense and myrrh were burned by rich people to freshen the air and hide body odor. They were also made into perfumes and ointments for the same purpose.

Frankincense and myrrh came from distant and mysterious places. They were scarce, expensive, and created white, pleasant smelling smoke. Soon they became associated with purity and immortality and took on religious uses. Both resins were burned in many cultures as offering to the gods. The Egyptians used myrrh to prepare mummies, and the Romans burned frankincense at funerals. Both resins became part of early Jewish temple rituals and were used regularly in the Christian church. Today, the Roman Catholic, Eastern Orthodox, and Anglican/Episcopal Churches still use these aromatic resins in some special rituals.

In ancient times, frankincense and myrrh were also used as medicines. Frankincense was thought to treat stomach problems and its oil to treat insect stings. In some cultures, it also was used as a cure for arthritis. Myrrh was

Did You Know?

In 65 CE, Nero, Emperor of Rome, burned Rome's entire year's supply of frankincense at the funeral of his second wife, Poppaea, in a show of great wealth and power.

used to treat wounds and mouth sores. Today it is still used in some mouthwashes.

Beyond their practical and religious uses, frankincense and myrrh became status symbols to the Romans. Welcoming guests by burning these resins showed that a family was wealthy. Frankincense and myrrh were given as gifts for the same reason. At one time, Romans spent more money on frankincense and myrrh than they did on all other spices combined. Historians estimate that at its peak, 300,000 tons of frankincense and myrrh moved along the Incense Route each year.

Economics of the Incense Route

The trade in frankincense and myrrh made many villages and traders rich. The value of these products was determined by supply and demand. Supply was limited. Trees that produced frankincense and myrrh grew only in a small area. Arab traders who used the Incense Route worked to keep the location of the trees secret so that they could control the supply of resin. They were so successful in misleading their customers that Herodotus, a Greek historian, wrote in the fifth century BCE that the frankincense trees

In many religions, including the Roman Catholic faith, incense is still used as an important part of rituals and celebrations.

were protected by flying snakes that could only be driven away by burning a magical substance known to local Arabs.

Demand for frankincense and myrrh was high in the Roman Empire, Greece, and throughout the Middle East. The resins were good products for trade. They did not spoil during their three-month journey along the Incense Road, and they were light in weight compared to their value. When demand was highest, their price at the end of the journey was one hundred times more than what traders paid the harvesters who collected the resin. One pound (.45 kg) of frankincense could cost more money than a farmer made in five years. The high cost and mysterious origins made frankincense and myrrh high status luxury items.

Traders who successfully made the journey along the Incense Route became rich, but so did villages along the Route. The traders spent money on food and shelter for themselves and their animals, bringing income into the villages. In addition, the tribes that controlled each region charged a *tariff* on every camel load of goods passing through their territory. Because water was available only at a limited number of places in the desert, traders had to stick to the Incense Route and could not take detours to avoid the tariffs.

As the villages along the Route grew rich, they built bigger buildings and complex irrigation systems to expand the area that could be farmed. Income from the traders also meant that people in the villages along the Route could buy goods such as wheat, wine, cloth, medicines, and copper and silver items that the traders acquired at the end of their journey and carried back with them to trade in Arabia.

The cycle of buying and selling along the Incense Route brought wealth to the Arabian Peninsula for hundreds of years. However, beginning about 300 CE conflict throughout the Middle East and poor economic conditions made trade on the Incense Route less safe and less profitable. Eventually many of the wealthy towns of Arabia faded into dusty ruins that are still being uncovered by archaeologists.

Text-Dependent Questions

1. Where did the Incense Route begin and end, and what modern countries did it cross?
2. What were some of the reasons frankincense and myrrh were so expensive by the time they reached customers in Rome?
3. Why were camels so important to trade in ancient times?

Research Project

The ruins of four ancient cities on the Incense Route in the Negev Desert—Haluza, Mamshit, Avdat, and Shivta— are on UNESCO World Heritage Sites. Look up the Negev World Heritage Site. Write a few paragraphs about the buildings found what they tell you about life in these cities.

The city of Bukhara, in present-day Uzbekistan, was a major cultural center of central Asia in ancient times, and an important stop on the Silk Road.

4

The Silk Route

T he Silk Route, sometimes called the Silk Road, was a network of trails that extended from China to the Mediterranean Sea. It got its name because silk from China was the most common and valuable product carried along the route. The Silk Route was the first complete route between the empires of China in the East and the Greek and Roman empires of the West. More than any other trade route, the Silk Route contributed to an exchange of cultures, technologies, arts, and religion as well as luxury goods.

Development of the Silk Route

The Silk Route developed in pieces over a long period until it eventually stretched 6,400 miles (10,000 km) from Changan (Xian) in northwest China, across deserts, mountains, and *steppes* until it reached Constantinople (Istanbul) in Turkey where it connected with trade routes going to Northern Europe. Pieces of the Route existed as early as 1500 BCE. Gradually these early trading paths were connected.

In the West by 450 BCE, the Persian Royal Road stretched 1,785 miles (2,860 km) from Smyrna (Izmir, Turkey) on the Mediterranean Sea to Susa (Shush, Iran). Persian king Darius I had the road built to improve communication within his large empire. Over time, the Persian Royal Road became part of the Silk Road. About 330 BCE, Alexander the Great, a Greek, conquered what is now Afghanistan and expanded the Greek empire as far as the Fergana Valley (modern Tajikistan and Kazakhstan). Alexander built roads to move troops and trade goods, but they stopped at the Tien Shan Mountains that rise as high as 24,400 ft (7,439 m).

Words to Understand in This Chapter

laquerware—a decorative item usually made of wood and covered with a protective coating of resin.

monopoly—a situation where one producer controls the entire market for a specific product.

porcelain—a type of ceramic material often used to make dishes created by baking clay and then glazing it with colored materials.

steppe—a large flat grassland with few trees similar to a prairie.

Zoroastrianism—a monotheistic (belief in one god) religion that was the official was the official religion of Persia (Iran) from 600 BCE to 650 CE. In 2015, there were about 190,000 people practicing Zoroastrianism worldwide.

A winding road snakes up the side of a mountain in the Tian Shan range, which separated the ancient civilization of China in eastern Asia from the civilizations in central Asia such as Persia and the Indus River valley. Over time roads such as this one were created to enable trade between these ancient civilizations.

On the other side of the mountains, China under the Han dynasty (202 BCE-220 CE) was experiencing a period of peace and prosperity. The Great Wall was repaired and extended. Soldiers patrolled the roads to keep traders safe from bandits. Trade throughout China increased and many cities became wealthy. However, expansion of trade routes to the west was blocked by the Tien Shan Mountains and the Takla Makan desert, an area 620 miles (1,000 km) long and 250 miles (400 km) wide. Here temperatures could reach 104° F (40 C), water was scarce, and sandstorms were common. The mountains and the desert were major barriers blocking trade and communication between East and West.

Despite these barriers, word reached Han Emperor Wu Di that people in the Fergana Valley, where Alexander the Great's roads ended, bred horses much bigger and stronger than the pony-sized horses that were raised in China at that time. In 138 CE, the emperor sent 100 men led by Chang

Chinese coins minted during the Han dynasty, which ruled China from 206 BCE until 220 CE. It was the Han rulers who sought to establish trade with the Persian and Roman empires.

Ch'ien to find out if these horses really existed. It took Chang Ch'ien 13 years to get to the Fergana Valley and back to China, and only one of the 100 men who went with him survived to return home. Chang Ch'ien reported that the large horses did exist. The emperor wanted to buy these horses for use in war. His interest in getting the horses stimulated the development of paths through the mountains and the desert. Soon the east and west parts of the Silk Route were connected. The route remained in use until about 1450 CE.

Travel on the Silk Route

Travel on the Silk Route was difficult and dangerous. In many places, the path was so narrow that a misstep could send man or animal sliding down the mountainside. Villages were far apart, and travelers often had to camp out in all kinds of weather. A shattered leg or serious illness meant death. Many men and animals died trying to cross the mountains or the desert. One Chinese traveler around 500 CE described the miserable experience this way. "There is snow both in winter and summer, winds, rain, drifting sand, and gravel stones. The road is difficult and broken, with steep crags and precipices on the way. The mountainside is simply a stone wall…on going forward, there is no sure foothold."

Traders traveled the Silk Route in large groups for safety. In good times, the government sent soldiers with them to protect them from bandits. Other times they hired their own guards or took the chance of being robbed and killed.

Silk Production

Silk fabric is made from the cocoons of a blind flightless moth, *Bombyx mori*. Each moth lays about 500 eggs and then dies. The eggs hatch into caterpillars that eat mulberry leaves (1). When the caterpillars are fully grown, they spin a thin strand of jelly-like material similar to a spider web around themselves to make a cocoon (2). In about nine days, that material hardens into silk. When the cocoons have hardened, they are dipped into hot water, and the white silk strand is unwound on to a spool (3). Each cocoon produces a single strand of silk 1,970 to 2,950 feet (600 to 900 m) long. Five to nine of these strands are twisted together to make silk thread that can then be woven into cloth (4).

The Chinese discovered the secret of silk very early and by 3000 BCE were "farming" silk under controlled conditions. The process was time consuming and required a lot of labor. One ounce (28 g) of silk moth eggs produced 30,000 caterpillars that ate about one ton (900 kg) of mulberry leaves and produced 12 lb (5.5 kg) of raw silk. Then more labor was needed to make the raw silk into cloth, dye it, and sew it into clothing. For many years the Chinese hid the secrets of silk production. This gave them control of the silk market and let them charge very high prices for silk cloth.

No one made the entire trip from China to Istanbul. Instead, a caravan from China would carry silk, jade, *porcelain*, *laquerware*, tea, and paper until it reached certain cities where other trading routes crossed the Silk Route. Here traders would barter or sell their cargo for items from the West such as glass containers, swords, perfume, horses, dates, pistachio nuts, spices, dyes, furs, gold, and silver. The Chinese traders would then turn around and take these goods back to their homeland, while their silk and other goods moved west along the Silk Route with new traders.

Between China and the countries around the Mediterranean Sea, goods changed hands many times, and the price increased with each exchange. Traders had to pay for food and shelter for themselves and their animal. They also had to pay taxes or tariffs to each local government or tribe that controlled an area. If they did not pay, their trade goods could be taken away from them. It could take three years and many exchanges for a cargo of silk to reach Rome. At the height of the craze for silk clothing, silk cloth sold in Rome for the equivalent of its weight in gold.

During the hundreds of years that the Silk Route was in use, the lands the Route traveled through were ruled by many different tribes and rulers. There were periods of peace such as during the Han dynasty when the trade in silk was at its height. During this time, the Han government policed kept the route safe from bandits. At other times, countries fought wars over control of the lands the Route crossed, and the trip was dangerous. The Route was closed several times for periods of many years. When there was

This minaret to a Muslim mosque in Xian shows distinctively Chinese architectural characteristics. Islam spread east into Central Asia and China during the eighth and ninth century by traders traveling along the Silk Route. Xian was a starting point for the trade route in China.

conflict, traders tried to find alternate routes to avoid bandits, battles, and outbreaks of disease.

Ideas Travel the Silk Route

Traders were not the only people to use the Silk Route. Soldiers, craftsmen, religious missionaries, artists, spies, and ordinary people looking for a better life all traveled the Route in both directions. They brought with them ideas, technology, and knowledge from their home countries. This great mixing of ideas helped to shape our modern civilizations. From China, people in the West learned papermaking, printing, and how to make porcelain, laquerware, and gunpowder. Spies sent from Constantinople (Istanbul, Turkey) traveled to China to steal silkworm eggs, breaking China's *monopoly* on silk production. From the West, people in China were introduced to glassmaking, new ideas about medicine, mathematics, and astronomy, and to new plants such as figs, grapes, and cucumbers. Artists borrowed designs from distant lands and added them to their own traditional work.

Religious ideas also traveled along the Silk Route. Buddhist monks, originally from India, were especially active along the trail. Dunhuang in northwestern China was once a major town

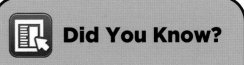

Did You Know?

The vast grasslands of the Central Asian plains provided fertile grazing and water for caravans. This enabled merchants to travel immense distances, from China to Africa and deep into Europe, without having to pass through farming communities, where they might have aroused suspicion and hostility.

The Mogao caves were a network of Buddhist temples located along the Silk Route. Today they are a popular tourist attraction.

on the Route. Near here, Buddhist monks between about 360 CE 750 CE carved 1,000 caves, called the Mogao Caves, out of rock cliffs. They decorated these caves with statues of the Buddha and paintings of daily life. The caves became a stopping place for traders on the Silk Route and helped spread Buddhist beliefs to Central Asia.

Today 735 caves still exist. The dry desert air has preserved the original artwork in these caves. The caves are

Tourists walk past ancient tile-decorated buildings in Samarkand. This city in central Asia is one of the oldest cities in the world. It was an important stopping point on the Silk Route for centuries.

Until 1877, the Silk Road or Silk Route had no special name. Ferdinand von Richthofen, a German geographer who made seven trips to China, was the first person to call it by a German term that translates into "Silk Road," and the name stuck.

protected as a UNESCO World Heritage Site. The Chinese government limits the number of people who can visit the caves each year in order to preserve them. Although the cave art survived hundreds of years in the desert climate, the moisture that visitors add to the air just by breathing is destroying the paintings.

Other religions also traveled the Silk Road. *Zoroastrianism* spread from Persia (Iran) west to India. Nestorian Christianity, a branch of the Christian church that believed Jesus was two people, one human and one divine, moved east along the Route. Out of the mingling of Buddhism, Zoroastrianism, and Nestorian Christianity, a new religion, Manichaeism, developed. Later Islam was introduced into Central Asia along the Silk Route. This mixing of ideas, cultures, and goods changed the way people thought about their world. It stimulated exploration, experimentation, and scholarship, and set the stage for our many of our modern ideas.

The Silk Route was at its best during times of peace and political stability. Around 1400, the Mongol Empire, which then controlled much of the Route, began to break down, and a series of local conflicts developed. Tension between Muslim and Christian countries increased to the point it was no longer safe for traders to use the Route. Meanwhile explorers had found sea routes between Europe and China. Trade by sea replaced overland trade, and the Silk Route fell into disuse. Today sections of the route in China from Changan (Xian) to the passage through the Tien Shan Mountains are protected as a UNESCO World Heritage Site.

 **Text-Dependent Questions**

1. Why was it so difficult to link roads in the East and roads in the West to make a continuous road for traders?
2. Name some trade goods that moved along the Silk Route from China to the Mediterranean region. What goods moved from the Mediterranean to China?
3. What kinds of ideas and information were spread by people traveling the Silk Route?

 **Research Project**

Marco Polo (1254-1324) left his home in Venice, Italy as a teenager and traveled the Silk Route all the way to China. He returned to Italy 24 years later, and his adventures were later published as a book. Many people refused to believe the stories of what he had seen were true. Research the life of Marco Polo and write a report on some of the new or surprising things he saw in his travels.

Some of the most valuable spices, including cloves and nutmeg, grew only in the Moluccas, a chain of volcanic islands in the Pacific Ocean between modern-day Indonesia and New Guinea that are also known as the Spice Islands. To reach markets in Europe and the West, these valuable goods had to be transported thousands of miles over the Spice Route.

5

The Spice Route

The Spice Route was a group of sea lanes that ships sailed carrying spices and other valuable trade goods between China, India, and the Mediterranean Sea, a distance of about 7,500 miles (12,000 km). These routes became important later than overland routes such as the Silk Route and the Incense Route, but remained in use into the sixteenth century.

Early Spice Trading

The Spice Route developed slowly, as small roads and trade routes, just as the Silk Route did. Although local trading among coastal communities in China began much earlier, regular sea trade between China and Korea was not established until the Han dynasty (202 BCE-220 CE). At the same time, the Koreans were trading with Japan. To ports in Korea, the Chinese took silk, cassia, ginger, jade, and iron. There they traded for Korean furs and goods from Japan to take back to sell in China.

During the Han dynasty, Chinese ships also sailed south along the coast of China and Vietnam to the Malay Peninsula, a thin strip of land that separates the Pacific and Indian Oceans. Here they traded for spices from the Moluccas, also known as the Spice Islands (now part of Indonesia). These small islands are located in the Pacific Ocean between the Philippines and New Guinea.

The Moluccas were enormously important to the spice trade. Until the mid-1850s, Banda, one of the Spice Islands, was the only place in the world to acquire nutmeg and mace. Other Spice Islands were the source of cloves. Spice traders tried to hide the existence of the Spice Islands by telling misleading tales about them, just as overland traders on the Incense Route had tied to hide the source of their trade goods. Later when Europeans found the Moluccas, they fought bloody battles for control of them because these

Words to Understand in This Chapter

cure (meat)—a way of preserving meat by spicing it or smoking it.

embalm—to use spices and chemicals to prepare a body for burial.

sea lanes—the ocean equivalent of land roads, sea lanes are routes regularly ships take across oceans. In ancient times, the sea lanes were determined by the strength and direction of the winds.

The word spice *comes from the Latin word species meaning an item of special value. At one time in Rome, black pepper was the most expensive spice in the world. Today the three most expensive spices are saffron, vanilla, and cardamom. These colorful spices are on sale at a modern souk (market) in Dubai, United Arab Emirates.*

spices were tremendously valuable.

Meanwhile, traders from India were sailing ships carrying cinnamon from Sri Lanka, a large island off the eastern tip of India, to ports on both the east and west sides of the Indian Peninsula. They also traded sandalwood (which was used as incense), lemon grass, ginger, and turmeric. Few ship captains were brave enough or foolish enough to cross the Arabian Sea to the west to reach Africa or cross the Indian Ocean to the east to reach the Malay Peninsula. It

This drawing from a 14th-century Arab book shows a dhow, *a vessel commonly used by Arab traders in the Indian Ocean. The ships were easy to maneuver because of their triangular sails—an innovation that European explorers soon adopted for their own ships.*

took the discovery of the monsoon winds to make open ocean voyages common.

The Secret of the Monsoon Winds

Before sailors discovered the secret of the monsoon winds, they were limited to carrying trade goods from port to port along the coast rather than directly crossing the ocean. The route was long and dangerous, and some spices spoiled on the way. It could take stops in many ports and two to three years for spices from Asia to reach Egypt, Rome, or Greece.

Ships in the ancient world were dependent on wind power to get from place to place. Discovering the pattern of the strong monsoon winds made it possible to sail longer distances across open ocean instead of staying within sight of land. The trip was still dangerous, but a round trip from China to the Middle East could be made in one year.

What makes the monsoon winds special for sailors is that they change direction in a regular way with the seasons. Monsoon winds always blow from a cold region toward a warm region. The change in wind direction happens in because the land heats up and cools down faster than the ocean. For example, from about April to

 Did You Know?

The Bactrian or two-humped camel is the toughest pack animal in the world. It can go without water for 40 days and withstand temperatures as low as -40°F (-40°C) in the winter and as high as104°F (40°C) in the summer. When water is available, it can drink 15 gallons (57 l) at a time. Without the Bactrian camel, traders could never have crossed the Takla Makan desert.

October, the Indian subcontinent heats up faster than the Indian Ocean, so winds blow from the cool ocean toward warmer India. From October to April, the land cools down

Spices of the Ancient World

Most of the spices used in the ancient world are familiar to us. In ancient times, these spices grew in only a few places. Today these spices can be farmed in many places with tropical climates, and they are no longer luxury goods available only to the wealthy.

Here is a list of spices that were in demand in the ancient world, where they came from, and how they were used in ancient times.

- Cloves are the dried flower buds of a tree that grew in the Spice Islands. They were used to *cure* meat, in cooking, and as a medicine.
- Ginger is the underground stem of a plant that grew wild in Java, India, and China. It is used as medicine and in cooking.
- Turmeric is the underground stem of a plant that grew in India and Indonesia. Besides being used in cooking, it was used to make a yellow dye.
- Nutmeg and mace come from the same tree. Nutmeg is the seed inside the fruit of the tree. Mace is a red lace-like mesh surrounding the seed. The tree grew only on Banda, one of the Spice Islands. Both spices were used in cooking and as medicine. Mace was burned as incense.
- Cinnamon and cassia are made from the bark of related trees. Cinnamon grew in Sri Lanka and cassia in Burma (Myanmar) and China. Both were used to *embalm* bodies, in cooking, and in ointments.
- Black pepper is the dried fruit of a flowering vine that grew on trees in south India. It was used in Egypt to prepare mummies and elsewhere in cooking.
- Cardamom comes from the seeds of a plant that grew in India and was used as a medicine and in cooking.

faster than the ocean, so the wind blows away from cooler India and toward the warmer ocean. In China, winter winds blow toward the South China Sea and the Pacific Ocean (toward Indonesia and the Spice Islands). In summer the winds reverse and blow toward the Chinese mainland letting ships complete a round trip. Once Arab and Indian sailors understood the regular pattern of the monsoon, they could time their trips to use the wind to sail across the Indian Ocean and up the Persian Gulf or the Red Sea and have access to the Mediterranean market. Chinese traders do the same for trips to the Spice Islands.

Control of the Spice Route

The spice trade was incredibly valuable. Wealthy people in Europe and the Middle East were crazy about spices. One historian estimates that in ancient Rome one pound (.45

This map shows the largest of the Spice Islands, between Sulawesi and New Guinea. Today, the islands are part of Indonesia. The Strait of Malacca, a passage between Sumatra and the Malay Peninsula, was a popular, though often dangerous, trade route.

Some people claim that the character Sinbad the Sailor, the hero of tales in the book One Thousand and One Nights, *was based on a real spice trader. To prove Sinbad's voyage was possible, a team from Britain and Oman built a* dhow *(boat) like Sinbad's. Using only the navigational instruments the fictional Sinbad would have had access to, they sailed from the Middle East to China. Their voyage took eight months.*

kg) of cinnamon sold for $409 in 2015 dollars ($545 Canadian). Pepper was worth so much to the Romans that peppercorns were used to pay rents, ransom, and tribute. When the Visigoths, an invading tribe, captured Rome in 410 CE, they demanded 3,000 pounds (1,363 kg) of pepper in ransom. Whoever controlled the *sea lanes* of the Spice Route would become wealthy and powerful.

The fastest, shortest way to sail from the Spice Islands to India and then on to the Middle East was through the Strait of Malacca. This is a narrow 550-mile (900-km) stretch of water that lies between the Malay Peninsula and the island of Sumatra. It is important because it connects the Pacific Ocean where the Spice Islands are located with Indian Ocean.

Beginning in about 800 BCE and for the next 250 years, the Strait of Malacca was controlled by the kingdom of Srivijaya from their city Palembang on the island of Sumatra (now part of Indonesia). The Srivijaya kingdom became extremely wealthy and powerful. The Arab and Indian traders who dominated the spice trade had to pay tribute in money or spices to pass through the Strait. Ships that would not pay were attacked by pirates who owed allegiance to the Srivijaya ruler. Although there were sea routes that avoided the Strait of Malacca, these routes were longer, more dangerous to navigate, and were also full of pirates. Most ships chose to pay to use the safer route.

The Search for Spices Drives Exploration

The spice trade continued even when wars broke out and empires fell. The leaders of the city-state of Venice (in present-day Italy) were especially clever at taking advantage of unsettled political times to gain a monopoly on the spice trade with Europe. Venice was a powerful seafaring city-state that had traded with the Arab world for many years. Beginning about 900 CE, the Venetians began making treaties with Arab rulers. Within about 250 years, they become middlemen in the spice trade between Arab traders and spice buyers in Europe. The treaties allowed the Venetians to buy all the spices the Arab traders brought to the Mediterranean region. The Venetians then turned around and sold the spices to countries in Europe at fantastically increased prices. No matter what other European countries tried, they could not break the Venetian's spice monopoly.

By the middle of the 1400s, European countries had begun searching to for a direct route to the Spice Islands in order to cut out the Venetian middlemen and bring down spice prices. In 1492, Spain sent Christopher Columbus to find India and the Spice Islands by sailing east across the

Portuguese warships sink an Arab freighter in the Indian Ocean during the early 16th century. The ruthless tactics of Vasco da Gama and other Portuguese mariners helped the tiny country gain control over the trade routes to the East Indies, bringing wealth and power to Portugal.

Atlantic Ocean. Instead, he found North America, although he thought he had found India, and called the Native Americans Indians. Five years later, Portuguese captain Vasco da Gama sailed around the tip of Africa and across the Indian Ocean to reach India. After that, the Venetian monopoly on spices was broken, and intense competition began among the Dutch, Portuguese, English, and Spanish to control the spice-growing regions of Asia.

 Text-Dependent Questions

1. What spices came from the Spice Islands?
2. Explain what monsoon winds are and why they were important to the spice trade.
3. Why was control of the Strait of Malacca so important to the spice trade?

Research Project

Choose a spice mentioned in this chapter. Research where it grows today and how it is harvested and prepared for sale. Find a recipe that uses this spice. If possible, ask an adult to help you make the recipe.

Chronology

~3200 BCE	Phoenicians arrive on the coast of Lebanon and establish city-states for trade.
~1200-800	Phoenicians are at their most powerful. They control much of the trade with countries bordering the Mediterranean Sea.
~800-550	The Strait of Malacca is controlled by the Srivijaya kingdom.
814	Phoenicians establish a trading colony at Carthage on the North African coast.
738	The Phoenician city-states fall under Assyrian rule, reducing their trading power.
700 BCE	The Incense Route is at its most active from this point until about 200 CE. Frankincense and myrrh move from Arabia to the Mediterranean region, commanding high prices.
~560	Buddha is born in Nepal.
538	The Persians conquer the Phoenician city-states. Many Phoenicians flee to Carthage, and Phoenician culture gradually dies out in the region of modern-day Lebanon.

484	Greek historian Herodotus is born. He is the first person known to systematically research historical information in an attempt to write an accurate history of the region.
450	The Royal Persian Road is completed from Smyrna (Izmir, Turkey) to Susa (Shush, Iran). This road forms an important link in the Silk Route.
330	Alexander the Great invades Afghanistan, building roads and bringing Greek knowledge and technology to the area.
202	The Han dynasty gains power in China. During Han rule, which ends around 220 CE, sections of the Silk Route are linked and peace and prosperity encourage Silk Route trade.
~1 CE	Buddhism begins to spread into Central Asia by way of trade routes. Silk reaches Rome from China for the first time.
31	Egypt becomes part of the Roman Empire, giving Rome access to new trade goods.
117	The Roman Empire reaches its greatest geographical extent, bringing standard weights and measures to a large part of Europe.
~220	The Han dynasty ends. China becomes fragmented by war, and trade on the Silk Route is disrupted.
~300	The Incense Route falls into disuse because of wars. Traders look for ways to move goods through the Red Sea.

Ancient silver denarius coins, minted in the Roman Empire.

~360	Buddhists begin carving out caves with elaborate paintings along the Silk Route, furthering the spread of Buddhism.
410	Rome falls to the Visigoths, a Germanic tribe. The days of spending huge amounts of money on luxury goods such as spices and silk end.
~500	Nestorian Christians reach China by way of the Silk Route, spreading their faith.

~700	Muslims control the Silk and Spice Routes. Islam spreads throughout the Central Asia and becomes the dominant religion of the region.
~900	The city-state of Venice, in Italy, makes treaties with Arab traders in order to establish a monopoly over the lucrative spice trade with Europe.
~1200	Paper money is introduced in Central Asia and slowly replaces gold and silver coins.
1271	Marco Polo sets off to travel the entire Silk Route to China, returning to Italy 24 years later.
~1450	The Silk Route is broken up by wars and no longer links China and the Mediterranean.
1492	Columbus tries to find a route to the Spice Islands by sailing west. Instead, he discovers the Americas.
1497	Portuguese captain Vasco da Gama sails around the Cape of Good Hope at the tip of Africa and across the Indian Ocean opening a new route to the Spice Islands and breaking the Venetian monopoly on the spice trade.

Series Glossary

barter—the official department that administers and collects the duties levied by a government on imported goods.

bond—a debt investment used by companies and national, state, or local governments to raise money to finance projects and activities. The corporation or government borrows money for a defined period of time at a variable or fixed interest rate.

credit—the ability of a customer to obtain goods or services before payment, based on the trust that payment will be made in the future.

customs—the official department that administers and collects the duties or tariffs levied by a government on imported goods.

debt—money, or something else, that is owed or due in exchange for goods or services.

demurrage—extra charges paid to a ship or aircraft owner when a specified period for loading or unloading freight has been exceeded.

distributor—a wholesaler or middleman engaged in the distribution of a category of goods, esp to retailers in a specific area.

duty—a tax on imported goods.

export—to send goods or services to another country for sale.

Federal Reserve—the central bank of the United States, which controls the amount of money circulating in the US economy and helps to set interest rates for commercial banks.

import—to bring goods or services into a country from abroad for sale.

interest—a fee that is paid in exchange for the use of money that has been borrowed, or for delaying the repayment of a debt.

stock—an ownership interest in a company. Stocks are sold by companies to raise money for their operations. The price of a successful company's stock will typically rise, which means the person who originally bought the stock can sell it and earn a profit.

tariff—a government-imposed tax that must be paid on certain imported or exported goods.

value added tax (VAT)—a type of consumption tax that is placed on a product whenever value is added at each stage of production and at final sale. VAT is often used in the European Union.

World Bank—an international financial organization, connected to the United Nations. It is the largest source of financial aid to developing countries.

Further Reading

Broida, Marian. *Ancient Israelites and Their Neighbors.*
Chicago: Chicago Review Press, 2003.

Major, John. *The Silk Route.* New York: HarperColllins,
1995.

Reid, Struan. *The Silk and Spice Routes: Explorations by
Sea.* New York: UNESCO Publishing, 1994.

Rodger, Ellen. *The Biography of Spices.* New York: Crabtree
Publishing, 2006.

Strathern, Paul. *The Silk and Spice Routes: Explorations by
Land.* New York: UNESCO Publishing, 1994.

Internet Resources

http://topdocumentaryfilms.com/the-frankincense-trail
A four-part BBC documentary on frankincense and the Incense Route.

http://whc.unesco.org/en/list/1107
Description of the remains of four ancient cities on the Incense Route declared protected as UNESCO World Heritage Sites.

www.silkroadfoundation.org
An extensive collection of maps, articles, and links about the Silk Road.

www.youtube.com/watch?v=j32yCYm6DFc
Secrets of Archaeology: Sailing with the Phoenicians is a video that summarizes the history of the Phoenicians and their contributions to civilization.

http://whc.unesco.org/en/list/440
A description of the Buddhist caves along the Silk Route and their significance to the spread of Buddhism in Central Asia.

Index

Numbers in ***bold italic*** refer to captions.

About the Author

Tish Davidson is an award winning author of 10 nonfiction books for children as well as many magazine and newspaper articles for adults. At home in Fremont, California, she and her family are volunteer puppy raisers for Guide Dogs for the Blind. Visit her at her website http://www.tishdavidson.com.